TIME 4 HEALING

(MAKE IT MAKE SENSE)

Time 2 MANning Up Series

Time 4 Healing
Copyright © 2023 by *Jasper Manning*.

Published in the United States of America
ISBN   Paperback: 979-8-89091-035-6
ISBN   Hardback: 979-8-89091-057-8
ISBN   eBook: 979-8-89091-036-3

All rights reserved. No part of this publication may be reproduced, stored in a retrieval system or transmitted in any way by any means, electronic, mechanical, photocopy, recording or otherwise without the prior permission of the author except as provided by USA copyright law.

The opinions expressed by the author are not necessarily those of ReadersMagnet, LLC.

ReadersMagnet, LLC
10620 Treena Street, Suite 230 | San Diego, California, 92131 USA
1.619. 354. 2643 | www.readersmagnet.com

Book design copyright © 2023 by ReadersMagnet, LLC. All rights reserved.

Cover design by Ericka Obando
Interior design by Don De Guzman

Time 4 Healing
(Make It Make Sense)
Time 2 MANning Up Series

Jasper "Mr. HORSE" Manning

TABLE OF CONTENTS

Preface ix
Affirmation The Healing Process x

CHAPTER ONE : SEE THE HEALING

The Great White Lie 2
A Handful of Man 4
Flash and Light 6
God Smiled 8
In Memory of 9
The Black Awakening 11
Blessed Nature 13
The Night Watcher 14
Black Forget Me-Nots 15
Moments of Discouragement 16
That Used to be Me 18
Talk to Me 20
The Mother of Days 22
Deja You(RAF Alconbury) 24
Grown Folks Stuff 26
Today I loss a Friend(10-09-2021) 28
Today an Angel Went HomeSept 15, 2021 30
Unknown feelings 32
A Brother Has Problems 33
Tears of angels 35
Worth the Wisdom 36
Hearts Do Not Lie 38
Scene Standing 40
Rise and shine 42

CHAPTER TWO: THAT HEALING TOUCH

A Good Heart 44
Strong enough 46
The Best Sleep In The World 48
Longevity's Brevity 50
Touched by Death 52
Today I Saw You 54
Golden Bear Pride 56
E. M. Daggett Bulldogs 58
Now and Next 60
That Little Girl Christmas Spirit 62
Things I Know About You 64
Hold On 66
Never Wishes 68
Shoulders and Sweethearts 70
When Luck Has Run 72
Christmas 2021 74
The Game of His Life 76
Internal Damage 78
It Could Have Been Me 80
Touch me, Heal me 83
Own Your Own Magic 85
Softer times 87
Acceptable 89
The Power of Prayer 91
Heaven's Lighthouse 93
We Gone Let It shine 95
Strong Who 97
Remember That Story 99
The Magic of Love 101

CHAPTER THREE: SMELL THE HEALING

When a fart is a fart 104
Adam and Eve(The Fall of Paradise)The Alternate Ending 105
My United States Air Force 108
The Privilege of Waking Up 110
Country Skies...112
Little Stinker 114
Names on God's List 116
Chose to Learn 118
Down Low 120
Through The Eyes of Hate 122
The Smell of Healing 124
That Last Breath 126
The Smell of Hickory...128

CHAPTER FOUR: TASTE THE HEALING

A Little Taste of Home 131
I Will Never Smile That Way Again 133
Eat to Live don't Live to Eat 135
The Favor to Savor 137
Easter Who 139
That Turkey on Thanksgiving 141
Quit It..143
The Inside Man..145
This Crazy Life...147
Life will Happen 149
Shrinage 151

CHAPTER FIVE: THE SOUND OF HEALING

Princess Sophia and Earl's Girl 154
In God's House 156
Silent Strength..158
That Old Couch 160
Candid Conversations 162
Mama Knew Something...164
That thing you do 166
Some People...168
When we Fellowshipped...170
Magical Moments 172
Speaking for a Friend 174
The Day You Became Who 176
A Family Thing 178
The Time I Needed God 180
A Song of Healing..182
Christian Expectation...184
Happy Employment...186
The Preovulation of GOD 188
Things I Can See — (May 10, 2022) 190
Who Knew...193
Who Has You...195
Ultimate Loss...197
The Other Side of Happiness 199
Non-Believers...201
A Father's Love 203
Strength for the Strong...205
Storybook Dreams..207
I was infuriated as an Educator..209
Day of Decency — December 16, 2021....................................211
Earlism (Part 3) 213

Final Thoughts...215
Index..217

PREFACE

This is the third edition in the book series of Time 2 MANning Up that began in November of 2019. The first book in the series was called Time 2 MANning Up. The recognition of American's and the issues that are encounter.

The first book was just another way to let the twelve tribes of Israel know, you are not alone in your fight. The second book in this series is called "America is Broken" which highlights the issues surrounding the life changing events of 2020. A time referred to as the twin year as defined by Michel de Nostradamus. Events that revealed the true fabric of America for all the world to see.

The third book is this series which is called ("HEALING" make it make sense). This third book in this series will hopefully provide additional gratification, spiritual motivation, and emotional support.

Affirmation The Healing Process

In order for the healing to begin
we must acknowledge the pain
the reason why this is important
is because the hurt had a name

Slavery murder and disrespect
All went hand in hand
God didn't create the privilege of white
That was created by man

Slavery is not something new
In fact it is very old
If you did know let the Bible show
Slavery was bandage we are told

Slavery is a part of our past
By tree and by sea we have died
Acknowledging those who passed
there are those who lied and some cried

Murder was here since the dawning of man
Let us look at Cain and Abel
He slew his brother for profit and gain
This is the Bible not just some fable

Take what they want when they want
Disrespect be it a woman or a man
Ranging from money drugs and property
A mule, and 40 acres of land

From our past time has amassed
Acknowledge the pain let's move on
A nation will not heal if we conceal
The hurt that still live in our homes

Chapter One

See the Healing

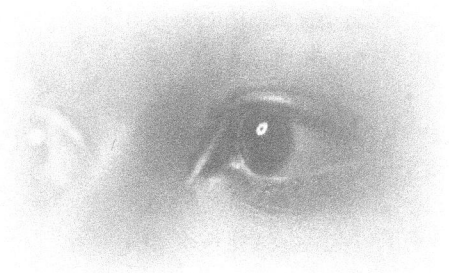

The Great White Lie

White is what they gave us to see
when Jesus looked like you and me
They couldn't control the narrative
So they gave us something to see

Lightening his skin, straightening his hair
We were not supposed to read
White is what they wanted us to see
If we are all awake then he could not lead

Hang white Jesus in the house
Hang a white Jesus on every wall
If we could not read the Bible
Then white Jesus is who we call

Kneeling to pray to white Jesus everyday
While a white man told us what to do
That narrative in mind it worked for some time
It was easier to control me and you

Now we must close our mouths
Close our minds don't believe what you read
God gave us the will to persevere
when we think God is planting his seed

Hair of wool skin of bronze
Is clearly what the Bible States
If you believe what they want us to see
Hopefully you won't wake up too late

It was all a lie in the by and by
White Jesus was all about control
Not able to read so they could lead
The WHITE Jesus narrative is old

Changing the color of his skin
To White so the world can see
The picture of a WHITE FACE JESUS
We know that thou art not thee

A Handful of Man

I can be a handful at times.
Get on my wife's last nerve
But at the end of each day
Treated as she deserves.

Requiring lots of attention
I guess any women will.
I knew the answer to that.
Before marriage sealed the deal

She is no walk in the park.
She has her moments as well.
She can be a downright grouch.
But understand I will never tell.

We have ups, and downs.
A life filled with positive stuff.
Her love for me is all I need.
My love should be enough.

We laugh before we go to bed.
Ninety percent of the time
When winding down it is found
I am hers and she is mine

I hear her voice on the phone.
And my day just takes a turn.
I will do what I can as her man.
To take care of her concerns

I would not trade her for the world.
And she feels the same way to
She knows with doors closed.
Together is what we do.

Flash and Light

Whenever tragedy tends to strike
There is a flashing of the light
Where times in life befall the eye
All the wrongs, all the rights

Events hit with a deep remorse.
If I could just do it again
Then the blessings show up
It had to be our God: Amen

Everything happens for a reason.
I have seen them firsthand.
If it had not been for our father
I would not be here as this man

God placed my name on a list.
So that I would wake up again
I am thankful in so many ways.
My road has not reached its end

If your life flashes before you
And you do not like what you see
Clapp your hands look to heaven.
And fall-down on your knees.

The light is there for a reason.
To guide you out of the dark
It will not stay on for too long.
You should embrace the spark.

I am grateful for my spark.
That led me from a place of dark.
Noah was crazy until it rained.
Now people could see the ARK.

God Smiled

While driving on the road one morning
After it had rained
Still the grass held water
It had not yet drained

The streets were slick
Yes they were somewhat wet
The rain finally stopped falling
But the storm wasn't over yet

The rain took his toll
As buildings begin to fold
Roofs caved in again and again
Structures were just too old

Wind would blow hail would fall
With a crystal covered ground
Thunder rolled as the storm grew old
Until there was little to no sound

The lightning stop the sun came out
As the day began to shine
Then over the sky God smiled
It was a rainbow a piece of mind

In Memory of

What is your in memory of
What will people think?
When no longer with this world
What will they see when they blink?

Will they see the changes in life?
That you help build in another
Or do they see the lack of effort?
Used to help a sister, or brother.

Will they see the life you lived?
Was an example of his word?
Will your memory be that of?
The sinful things they heard.

You create your memory of
With what you are doing today
Live your life in a manner.
That will inspire from what people say.

When people tend to mention your name
Are faces blessed with a smile.
Because the efforts of your good deed's
Live one for miles and miles

So, when people reflect in life.
Will hearts be full of love?
The mere mention of you
Is who there are memories of

The Black Awakening

Finally the real awakening
Colonizers and a bed of lies
They kill, lie, steal, and cheat
Then again this is no surprise

The real surprise is taking a people
To change the color of their skin
Make them think they are white
To control them from within

The 12 tribes Of Israel
Spread throughout the lands
Still wanting to whitewash history
Stay asleep, so you do not understand

The Israelites were black people
The Hebrew people were too
Telling the world the world is white
That's what some white people do

The real aloof is the lack of truth
The disciples of Christ were black
Bible depictions hidden in diction
That intelligence is what we lack

Black women carry the Eve gene
Creating the color of many
If we did not migrate to the north
White people there would not be any

A black statue of Jesus Christ
Was hidden away in Greece
Destroy our minds, we don't shine
Colonizers stealing our peace

If you look from the inside out
There is no color in blood type
If no one knows let me disclose
The color thing would be no hype

Who knows down-the-line what we find
Hidden away from the lot of you
Conventions of intentions to deceive
I am Jasper Manning, guess what,
                      I am black to.

Blessed Nature

The middle of the night
And the twinkling of the stars
The sounds of nature
No trains planes or cars

Just the sound of crickets
And animals moving about
Were the night lights up
And the bugs never go out

Where the breath of life
Rides the midnight dew
And it seems as if the world
Was put here just for you

Close your eyes open your mind
Then open your nose
Challenge your mind all the time
And yes just suppose

What would happen
If there were no stars no skies no seas
When nature didn't have to be
Guess what, neither did we

The Night Watcher

As I watch over thee
No harm shall come to thee
For as I watch over you
God watches over me

Where rest is endured
Peaceful is thy sleep
With your life I will protect
In my hands I will keep

Wipe your eyes when you cry
Wake you when you weep
Help you understand your dreams
When disturbed is your sleep

Wipe your sweat when it is hot
Cover you when it's cold
For sleep is our silent escape
Dreams began to unfold

As I watch over thee
No harm will come to thee
While I watch over you
God watches over me

Black Forget Me-Nots

I haven't forgotten what it took
To be where I am today
I haven't forgotten about the dreams
Of ancestors from yesterday

I haven't forgotten about the boat
Bringing us to the land of opportunity
I haven't forgotten about the denial
Of our lives liberty and equality

I haven't forgotten about the people
Who died while planting seeds
I haven't forgotten sacrifices made
So I could learn how to read

I haven't forgotten about the blacks
Hanged by the neck from trees
I will never forget the roots of prayer
Whenever I am on my knees

Life wasn't fair for black's back then
And still it's not better yet
I haven't forgotten what it's like to be black
And I never will forget

Moments of Discouragement

Every now and then discouragement
Will rear its ugly head.
Instead of trying to find the answer.
People give up instead.

You are not in a leadership role.
But your characteristics are strong.
Following behind a bad leader
Will make and short day long

Things that are demotivating
That brings the entire staff down
Feeling defeated deep inside
A paycheck is why they are around.

Our children will suffer in the end
When there is nowhere to turn
Inside their eyes is filled with cries
Life is what they must earn.

Failing to take the necessary steps.
When that education was free
The basic things they need in life.
Is hiding where they can see.

How do you shine a light?
Inside of an empty room
Help them cope, give them hope.
The possibilities of life loom

It is hard for a winner to quit
Pressing on is what we will do.
When discouragement rears its head
Do not let discouragement discourage you.

That Used to be Me

Not too long ago
I used to be a child
Doing childish things
Playing football in the streets
Shooting baskets
Through a bicycle ring

Cutting and trimming bushes
While mowing
And raking the lawn
We would play
In the streets for hours
From sun down to dawn

Yeah we looked
Under little girl's dresses
And pull chair from under kids
It was a part of growing up
Getting in trouble
For the things we did

Now as a man
I'm all grown up
Trying to raise two sons
Now I get so much joy
and pleasure
Watching them play and have fun

It is hard enough
To be an adult
Even harder now to be a kid
I try to be fair
But disciplined as well
I think about things that I did

They ran through the house
Bumping furniture and
knocking over glass
They would play outside
Wet or dry
Tracking mud dirt and grass

When they do wrong
I try to hold on
And see from what they see
When they grow up
With memories in their cup
I can say that used to be me

Talk to Me

I wish I had a me.
That I could talk to
Someone with some insight
That can give me a clue

I would not have to think twice.
What the advice I would give?
Then I would use that advice
Tell me, how would you live

I would look into the future.
Prepare myself for a heart break.
But do not forget never to fret.
God will provide the answer so wait.

Stocks would hit an all-time low.
You should invest.
Oil stocks USO and CPE
In June 2020 out-perform the rest.

If I had me to talk to
What else would I have to say
I would say to say to my dad.
I will love you dad anyway.

If I could talk to me
Some decisions would have changed.
Just so I can end up here
Enough to wipe away the strange

If I could talk to me
My mom would be alive today.
It is why I cannot hear my guy.
God wanted it that way.

Since I cannot talk to me
God is my next choice
Even though I say nothing.
He can still hear my voice.

The Mother of Days

This day I visited my mother
I finally found the strength
I had to search for her headstone
It would take the morning at length

There were other Alice's
I wonder who could they be
Did they mean as much to theirs
As my Alice meant to me

Jerry took one side of the graveyard
And I took the other
We search that side of the graveyard
But still couldn't find my mother

A kind lady appeared to ask
Need help finding someone today
Yes we're trying to find my mother
Her name is Alice Faye Ray

We finally found her grave site
Were they placed my mother's remains
There stood this mom's headstone
That held my mother's name

I tipped my hat to think her
For helping me become a man
With all the things she did for me
I was now able to understand

Jerry ask if I was alright
Then I replied everything is okay
He looked at me and took my hand
And said come on man let's pray

He said a prayer and thanked the Lord
For the lives my mom touched
He said the things I would have said
He knew I missed her that much

When his prayer have reached an end
I placed flowers in a new hole
Then we turned and walked away
Rest in peace mom, God bless your soul

Deja You
(RAF Alconbury)

Have you ever ran into someone
Who smile was so contagious
They can take the simplest things
And make them seem outrageous

When they laugh you laugh
The expression on your face change
Laughing for no reason at all
Leaves to question of being deranged

All they do is catch an eye
When walking through the mall
Smiles are all over the place
With laughter big and small

Or at an Alconbury reunion
Friends for over 30 years
Things amidst you still miss
Laughing yourself into tears

Their energy and their vibe
Happens all over again
The things that set you apart
Now just end in Amen

There are times in a life
That stay as you move on
To you surprise you realize
That time was never gone

A used to be dap now overlaps
That rolls into a meaningful hug
You are here God was clear
The heart now has a grateful tug

You now go back to your lives
Only again to count the days
Hopes within, see each other again
Gives us another reason to pray

Grown Folks Stuff

Getting old sucks
but not everyone has the chance
sooner or later we walk the walk
and dance our own dance

Life begins to look different
with every passing day
A deeper appreciation for life
Value added to your way

Arguing can be meaningless
but necessary at times
People don't understand simple
So, invite them into your find

They may not see it now
but later it will come to light
Words spoken left darkness
When older will soften the night

I used to be that younger person
living my life my way
Now that I am getting older
I revere the time of each day

TIME 4 HEALING (MAKE IT MAKE SENSE)

I used to make old folk jokes
Keep living life young man
I would here this time after time
Now I truly understand

I want to thank my mom
God and I have a relationship
She knew things I didn't know
Prayer strengthens love ship

Never take for granted
Each and every passing day
You can make fun of us now
Your dance is on the way

The older in life you tend to get
The more you tend to see
I guess that's how it's always been
and how it will always be

Today I loss a Friend (10-09-2021)

Friends will not see the day out.
As I can see a new day in
God has blessed my wife and I
To breathe another breath again

Don died on the basketball court
Doing something he loved
Refereeing basketball games
Living the life, he dreamed of

You can tell how a person lived.
By the way that people leave
People need time to embrace loss.
As they take time to grieve

Longevity is the life you live.
Giving you more people to know
To see them filled with so much life.
Just to see them lose that glow.

It causes me to reflect on life
And the contributions I make.
How much fun you put in life.
And seriousness of life you take.

We conversed about our kids.
His daughter and my son
Look at where they are now
Compared to where they begun

At moments you heart takes a dip
Then peace of mind brings it back
What you learn from the loss
Gives your life a brand-new act.

There were times you laughed
And invited a serious word.
Words based on life experiences.
And not something you heard.

You saw them in passing.
Having kind things to say
God calls them home.
You are reminded of a day.

Tears filled the wells of my eyes.
Not because I was stressed.
Tears turn to cry's when friends die.
Tears because I am blessed.

Today an Angel Went Home
Sept 15, 2021

My second mom passed today
and she's gone just like that
she will definitely be missed
This one hit hard, to her I tip my hat

She wasn't afraid to tell me
the things I needed to hear
Living her life through Jesus Christ
No worries and no fear

She always had a conversation
Ready to give some advice
if you were wrong she told you
she didn't even think twice

In her I was able to confide
In 1997 when my mother died
Again tears stained my face
With eyes closed I still cried

A stranger never left her house
Once you walk through her doors
If you entered an empty vessel
Her wisdom left you wanting more

When my wife and I would visit
We would cut up talk and share
She always spoke from her heart
And yes Uncle Fletcher was there

Jasper you should know better
The times when I made mistakes
Your mom would turn over in her grave
and for me that is all it takes

Whenever I would leave her house
I was better than I went in
She was not just my aunt
She was another voice within

God has picked another flower
An angel is on her way home
Say hello to my mother
Now momma is no longer alone

Unknown feelings

Empathy for others
The greatest trait of all
To feel someone else's pain
And understand why they fall

To know what others go through
Whenever ends don't meet
To find a way to take their place
But there are shoes won't fit your feet

You cry their cries
And weep their woes
It's hard for people to understand
Because nobody knows

What must occur for them
In order to achieve success
Each situation is unique
Separating them from the rest

Empathy is a feeling
Hard to understand but real
God goes through this everyday
Can you imagine how he feels

A Brother Has Problems

A brother cannot get any love
    What are morning's is made of

Brother can't get no sleep
    That's the lay of the week

Brother can't get no time
    He's always on the grind

Brother can't get no cuddle
    Left in his mind to muddle

Brother can't get no cheese
    Even if he's asking please

Brother can't get no taste
    Wow that woman is a waste

Brother can't get no prayer
    Because the knee is not there

Brother can't get no stay
    Because he's always away

Brother can't be made
    Because of all the shade

Brother can't get rest
    Because of all the stress

Brother just can't win
    Because of the hater within

A brother is in despair
    In his mind he cannot share

Tears of angels

A drop of rain
Falls from the sky
Is what we reap
When angels cry

Snow is their cereal
That the heavens eat
But it covers the ground
Our hands and our feet

When it rains
People say it pours
It is God washing the wounds
Of nature's open sores

Then the sun comes out
As the healing begins
Man found a way to mess it up
So, we start all over again

That is why rain drops
From the heavens fall
Because angels from above
They weep for us all

Worth the Wisdom

Some people leave impressions
before they leave this earth
you don't know until they go
truly what they were worth

Dropping those subtle sayings
That remain with you today
"God don't like ugly"
Repeating what they would say

"Experience is your best teacher"
Hattie Mae miles and Clan
if you did not know Hattie
then you would not understand

"Don't wear out your welcome"
Is what Mom used to say
As I am grown I pass it on
It still lives with me today

Know that Fast is overrated
Slow was always better
When the mouth goes south
Slow down, get it together

Yes wisdom aligned with worth
is what Elders leave to us
Take your time to slow the mind
There is a lot in life to discuss

Hearts Do Not Lie

If your heart had a voice
What prêt ail would it say
I miss you when I am not with you.
Every moment of the day

I want to hold you when you cry.
So, you do not feel alone.
Protect you when you fall asleep.
Till your worries are gone

I enjoy the way you touch me
As special as it may be.
When we sigh as the moon passes by
That time is fine with me

Would it say that I am upset?
So, we can work things out.
So, you will have no need to go.
That is what this heart is about.

We would say with passive emotions.
I am so glad that you are here
I love the way love each other.
By day, by the week, and the year

The heart detector tells the truth
Because hearts do not lie
Learning to love and forgive.
As time slowly passes by

Finally, but not least of all
Thank you for protecting me.
You will do for me what I do for you.
That is the way love should be.

Scene Standing

Fall scenes
Winter scenes
Grass turns brown
After turning green

See the dead
See the mundane
See flowers and trees
Blossom when it rains

Spring scenes
Summer scenes
Times of the year
Where magic is seen

See people enjoy
What nature has to offer
Living life fancy free
Soft water becomes softer

See birds find a reason
To sing at morning time
Kids spend money for treats
Laffy taffy was a dime

Life is like a TV show
Everyone has a part
Dad out cutting the yard
Pouring into home his heart

Mom is inside cooking
Relaxing in the breeze and sun
Kids playing tag outside
Laughing while they run

Life can be exciting
Life can truly be grand
When you know in life
Where it is you stand

Rise and shine

You have to get up rise and shine
When people knock you down
You shouldn't stay there alone
You might get use to the ground

First you must build-up speed
Try not to lose momentum
People don't want to see you finish
Especially ahead of them

Even when the line is crooked
You have to straighten it out
Continue to walk through doors
When people push you out

Making breaking opportunities
Even when your world seems blue
You have to maintain your focus
When others can't adjust their view

People will try to push you down
While digging up dirt to find
No matter how many times you fall
You must rise one more time

Chapter Two
That Healing Touch

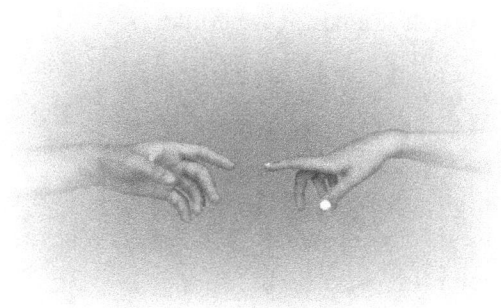

A Good Heart

Today was A-day like any other day
My son and I had no school
So we took this time together
To just hang out and be cool

We decided to take in a movie
Action packed and it was good
One fight scene after another
We'd watch it again if we could

So we took a walk outside
Then decided to take a drive
Man with one deep breath
I thought it is good to be alive

My son and I sat idly by
Waiting for our lunch that day
With rib tips and fried chips
We had lunch with nothing to say

My son and I enjoyed the meal
Now it was time to go
I received a mint my son a balloon
Before we walked out the door

There's nothing like time we'll spent
With time for a father and son alone
My son told me he loved me that day
When we were on our way home

Then my son asked a question
In the middle of this afternoon
"Dad can I give God a gift?" Sure
Then he set free his balloon

Strong enough

Strong enough to lead
Strong enough to follow
Strong enough to pride
Strong enough to swallow

Strong enough to day
Strong enough to night
Strong enough to wrong
Strong enough to right

Strong enough to laugh
Strong enough to cry
Strong enough to leave
Strong enough to die

Strong enough to teach
Strong enough to learn
Strong enough to work
Strong enough to earn

Strong enough to silence
Strong enough to pray
Strong enough to hear
Strong enough to say

Strong enough to self,
Strong enough to be alone
Strong enough to pain
Strong enough, own your own

Strong enough to stay
Strong enough to leave
Strong enough to compromise
Strong enough to believe

Strong enough to sit
Strong enough to stand
Strong enough to woman
Strong enough to be a man

The Best Sleep In The World

The best sleep in the world
Is sleep right after sex
Sleep in the middle of the day
Is what a time to pick to rest

Fall asleep on the couch
In front of the television set
Only to wake a few minutes later
And find the game isn't over yet

Rest while someone else is driving
Reclined back in the passenger seat
Doze off gazing through the roof
Disturbed by rain's gentle beat

Fast asleep on a Sandy beach
Threw the toes roll a cool breeze
Sleep while resting in a lawn chair
The sound of wind battling leaves

Falling asleep in the church
While the pastor is preaching
Awaken from laughter in class
While the teacher is teaching

The sweetest sleep anyone can reap
Comes from little boys and girls
Sleeping without worry or care
The best sleep in this whole wide world

Longevity's Brevity

There is a price for longevity.
People will die before you do.
They come they go nothing to show.
But they get to leave before you.

If they are a part of your life
Then the hit is first-hand
One day here the next day gone.
You are trying to understand.

Flooding the eyes with tear drops
Water from the stream of hearts
It all ends with the death of friends.
Friendships a place where it starts.

Then what of the people who leave
With not so much fun for fondness
They leave too right in front of you.
Do you grieve anything less?

With living a long life
You have some stories to tell.
Embracing happy times on earth
People live their lives and oh wells.

As you continue to rise up
People continue to lay it down
Living life through pain and strife
One day you will cover the ground

Touched by Death

What once moved freely
Now just lies still
Her skin was very cold
Yet the moment was real

Her eyes were closed
As if in a deep sleep
Mom is gone forever
Not the next day or week

I touched her face
I touched her eyes
For I know she relieved
And again will never cry

Her head would never ache
Her body is in no more pain
God leaned over her that day
And called my mother's name

Her hands were hard
And her finger tips white
I still see her face at times
When I'm asleep at night

My heart at times beat fast
And eyes would sometimes tear
Life now has new meaning
For in death I have found fear

Not the fear of dying
But of not being ready to die
For those we leave behind
Should never wonder how or why

As mom lies still
Her soul has been released
When I looked upon her face
All I can see is peace

Today I Saw You

Today, when I woke up.
The day, blessed with your smile.
Stretching to yawn from the dawn.
The stretch went on for a while

You mustered up the energy.
To say, "Hey good morning boo"
Our hearts blessed by love.
One of the things we say and do.

Throughout the day
I find myself singing certain songs.
Songs we hear when alone.
Telling us about life, where we belong

After our discussions at night
Songs at times will reiterate.
We can surpass the meaningless
To live life and be great

Before we head off to work
Before we walk out of the door
Holding each other for the first time
Like we have never kissed before

Taking to the world unknown
Until we see each other again.
Closing our eyes, we summarize
We embrace where it all began

Thanking God who carried us through.
This life of love and happiness
Morning, and noon consumed.
I feel like I am the one whose blessed

Golden Bear Pride

If you attended South Oak Cliff
It was in our nature to compete.
We did not experience allot of loss.
We just never expected defeat.

If given another chance
We would play to make amends.
It would never be personal.
We just had to be the best and WIN

You would never understand.
If you did not attend the school
Winning was not just a standard.
Simply put, it was a personnel rule

At times loss would cross our lips
The taste would never last long
In the next competitive match up
That taste was already gone.

Remembering what it tasted like
From the quiet bus ride home
Practice and preparation intense
The top has always been our throne

So, whenever we would win.
The result is what we expected.
Although we would taste a loss
Our presence, always respected.

Pride and Excellence
The embodiment of a Golden Bear
You will never understand the stand.
Unless you taught or attended school there.

*Dedicated to the Alumni of
South Oak Cliff High School*

E. M. Daggett Bulldogs

I once coached a group of girls.
And guys along the way
They started out as puppies.
And became Bulldogs one day.

Buying into the arduous work
Pride would then set in
Whenever they hit the floor
Losses turned into wins.

I did not just have two sons.
I inherited daughters as well.
My family began to extend.
My son's had brothers as well.

We opened the gym for growth.
Then had to kick the out.
Excepting discipline when wrong
Is what family being all about?

All the laps around the school
Then push-ups on my count
A scoreboard lit they never quit
Until it was time to dismount

Growing as Bulldogs then they left
Passion showing through play.
Married becoming mom's and dad's
Raising their children that way

I will be forever grateful.
They let us lead them in play.
Daggett Bulldogs in life forever
Tomorrow, yesterday and today

Becoming young men and women
Making up their own minds
Winning on the court is winning in life.
Not just their dream but mine

Now and Next

First you have the now,
Then you have the next
If you struggle prioritizing
This can be complex.

Know what to do now.
And what to do later
Fighting decisions of the mind
The girlfriends and the haters

You have lived for the now.
With the next never a thought
Never worried about saving
What you have is what you brought

Never having to change a flat
Or put gas in a car.
There is more to vehicle maintenance.
Then gas and air by far

You always play the catchup game.
Instead of being ahead
You will never be able to save.
If you are always in the red

God did not intend for us to struggle
A life of meaning fulfilled.
Work hard every day just to pay your way.
Sit back relax, life signed and sealed.

If you continue to think about now
Then the next will be the never
If we do not set goals for the next
Then now will be forever.

That Little Girl Christmas Spirit

Just a kid at heart
But adult was she in mind
Exposed to life events.
Before it was her time

She will never have a chance.
To relive that age again
Hopefully, she will meet someone
Who will help her understand?

Watching her during a Christmas show
She was dancing in her seat.
God bless this little girl's heart.
She never skipped a beat.

Rudolph this, and Rudolph that
Reindeers and a shiny nose
Smiles for miles, and miles, and miles
Until the concert closed

She returned true to form
With that mouth and that attitude
Same old smart mouth
Again, this student was rude

We should get Christmas songs.
And play them all year long.
The only time of the year
Where she feels she belongs

Trapped in a little girl's body
A child thinking, she is grown.
I hope and pray she finds a way.
The day she lives on her own.

Things I Know About You

I know that when I see you
My heart warms my soul
I know that when I'm with you
The day quickly grows old

I know that when you smile
The whole world smiles back
I know that when you walk
I am fine with how your body acts

I know that when I touch you
Your panties become wet
I know that when we kiss
There are things we both forget

I know that when I taste you
My appetite will longs for more
I know that if you taste me
There will be no time before

I know that when you're excited
Your body feels relieved
I know that doing our act of love
Our bodies can hardly breathe

I know with each passing day
When I rise I think of you
Grateful we belong to each other
Intimately I am with you

I know when you're away from me
There is a part of you I miss
I know that when we are together
We create moments to reminisce

Hold On

Things you cannot hold young or old.
Before their hold time comes to past
You can try to hold your breath at times
But hold time will not let it last

Try to hold a yawn from deep within
When it comes it will have its way?
Understood the yawn is good.
If your body has something to say

You can hold a balloon not tied off.
But eventually your fingers get tired.
You can hold your praise most days
Until the message leaves you inspired

You can hold on to good things
If you chose to respect what is serves
Like two people in a beautiful relationship
At times testing, each other's nerve's

Vows in a marriage hold a bond.
That two people share for life
In thick-n-thin hold vows within
So, do so as Husband and Wife

You can hold on to grudges at times.
But who does the grudge affect?
If what they do seems to irritate you
Then the grudge has your respect

If grudges consume and present gloom
It may be time to let the grudge go.
Peace within intend to live again.
But not if that grudge has a say so

Never Wishes

I never wished to be something else.
Or be like my friends.
All I want is to be J. Earl Manning
Until the very end

I never wanted to be a Rockefeller
Although it would be nice
That means I would need to reincarnate.
I would have to live twice

I never wished to be a pro athlete.
I am fine with what God made.
I will not hate on my fellow man.
I have never thrown shade

I never wished to live forever.
Through God my life has meaning
Like Dr. King, I have dreams
With a strength to survive my esteem

Never wished I had a mistake.
That I could do over again
Learning lessons taught
It is why I am my own man

I never wished my life turned out.
Differently from what it did
I remember people who touched my life
From the time that I was a kid

I never wished my mom did not die.
God new I would be good
I never wished my sons were me.
One day they will stand for what I stood.

Shoulders and Sweethearts

If I could sit on your shoulder
And whisper in your ear
You would laugh and be amazed
By the sentiments you would hear

You would stare and shout in awe.
With the things I would say
Because I would point out things
People do not notice everyday

I would tell you that I love you
In a different language everyday
Spanish, Chinese, and Italian
Then language from around the way

Knowing that you would have to go.
When really you wanted to stay
Work is a natural part of life.
But love helps us through the day.

I would tell you your breath stinks.
Or how nice you really smell.
People would wonder why you smile.
If you do not, then I will not tell.

That there is a little man
Sitting on your shoulder at times
I think of you as quiet as kept.
You are on these shoulders of mine.

When Luck Has Run

While driving down the street
A dog stood amiss a curb
I saw him trembling at the paw
It must have been his nerves

He stood as if to count cars
Contemplating weather to cross
When I looked into his eyes
I could see his spirit was lost

Just before the intersection
He lunged into the street
Jamming my car's emergency brake
I got out, he stood at my feet

I thought he would cross the street
Disappointed he turned and went back
I think his original intent that day
Was to leave this world on his back

There he stood on the curb
Missing patches of hair from his mane
Only walking on three of his legs
The dog didn't answer to any name

He appeared there on that curb
Waiting for another car to pass
Hoping maybe his luck would run
Or praying that it wouldn't last

I wondered what could be so bad
That this dog would want to die
Just like people you never know
When you look into their eyes

Christmas 2021

Christmas 2021 this year
Will have a different feel.
My Dad and Aunt Pearl are gone.
It just does not seem real.

Shopping will be different.
No slippers and no robe
No drive to pleasant grove
Life has taken a different road.

The E.F. Hutton's of my life
Will no longer have a say.
Their words of wisdom spoken
Will have a place of stay.

My heart had empty spaces.
Now there are two more.
Spaces marked by elders.
Leaving me keys to the door

Words spoken are the keys.
For families, to led by
I will pass on these keys.
Until it is my turn to die

I will miss the phone calls.
Of man what about this
He never chose for me.
His guidance we will miss.

Then I will miss Aunt Pearl
The bible was her guide.
Living life without worry or strife.
She left this world with pride.

Thankful for this Thanksgiving
And all it continues to bring.
Christmas 2021 this year
Will be a new kind of something.

The Game of His Life

A young man's dad died before
The day of a tie breaker game
I know from personal experience.
His life will never be the same.

They cancelled the game that night
Only to play the following night
This young man suited up to play.
Not knowing his head was right.

He had the game of his life.
The game of his life was on hand.
Both teams prayed before the game
Loss is something everyone understands.

He made things happen.
That forged his team to win.
He did not just do it once.
He did it time, and time again

They never trailed during the game.
As the other team would attack
The game ended, the ball in his hand
Tears, the thing he could not hold back

His performance was epic this day.
As his father watched from above
As he cried in the middle of the court
Both teams showed him love

As a ref I exited the court
Amazed at what just took place.
To my surprise from my eyes
Tear tracks appeared on my face.

Dedicated to Abdurahman Hammad
Brighter Horizon Academy 2022

Internal Damage

When you heat damage is internal
One might think computer parts
Something is not working right
Beginning from the click start

The screen may go black, flutter
Or the buffering prompt comes on
Either way it's hard to sit and stay
You didn't want to be there that long

You might think of an automobile
After it was in a wreck
The outside has minimal damage
Internal is what the adjuster inspects

People can have internal damage
not seen from the outside
Their hurting parts have hurt parts
A smile is how they hide

You don't see the hurt when dating
Feelings and emotions are knew
You enjoy the time shine your shine
The hurt affects them and you

People will abandon the relationship
And not think a second thought
I just cannot deal with this mess
While marriage and kids are bought

If you want to keep what you have
Then deep is where you must dig
You cannot cover it up with bandages
And you cannot hide it under a wig

You have to ask hard questions
Tell me something about you I don't know
And if they're true to themselves and you
Sit back and watch as the hurt flows

Now you have to decide
Should you go or do you ride
Do you help repair what is internal
So it starts to look like its outside

You've spent all of this time
To make this person your mine
You decide to stay there will be a day
That you will become their mine

It Could Have Been Me

It could have been me.
Out there in the streets
Mom working two jobs.
To put shoes on our feet

It could have been me.
Hanging from a tree
Born the right time right place.
Grace is all I can see.

Our mom did her best
To give us what we had
That was my life growing up.
Without the presence of dad

It could have been me.
Living in the projects
But mom made sacrifices.
That gave us her respect.

Church was our Sunday's.
Sunday school and the choir
Greater New Friendship Baptist Church
Became our hearts desire.

It could have been me.
Being-jumped, into a gang
Easter Sunday, Mother's, day
And Christmas songs we sang.

It could have been me.
Skipping school and class
It could have been me
With the police on his ass

It could have been me.
Locked up behind bars.
It could have been me.
Late at night stealing cars

That could have been me.
God had a different plan.
Making sure it would not be me.
Mother's hand used as God's his hand.

 It could have been me.
Kids all over the place
It could have been me.
That street violence erased.

It could have been me.
With drugs and the weed
Placing blame on everything else
For why I could not succeed

TIME 4 HEALING (MAKE IT MAKE SENSE)

At age 22 here comes dad
Taking up mom's slack
Teaching me to be a man
And how a man should act.

Yes, that could have been me.
The Black men that I see.
Falsely accused and abused.
God made sure it was not me.

Touch me, Heal me

Has anyone ever touched you
and it made everything okay
their touch said a lot more
than any words could say

Touched you on your shoulder
And it seem to calm you down
Walked this land hand in hand
and safe is what you found

Ran fingers through your hair
and chills rushed your spine
it may not do it for you
but that's what it did for mine

touched you on your leg
when anxious is what you felt
Touched a place the smile on your face
You know the heart would melt

then there's that touch
that did not feel so good
a touch meant to protect you
Didn't feel the way it should

Then there is the shoulder
you find when you need to cry
releasing tears from your fears
Finding the answers to why

Then there is the touch from God
that will place the body at ease
a touch that is so consuming
it brings you to your knees

thank you God for mercy
and for b watching over me
touch me anytime I need it
With you is where I want to be

Own Your Own Magic

Everyone will not be an idol
Nor have that special voice
You can always choose to be you
Always have that choice

Everyone won't drop a basket
Or carry players across hey goal line
They won't use a hockey stick
Or be the first across the finish line

Not everyone can rap a lyric
or dance their way to a video
If you fail to choose your magic
What will you have to show

Swimming laps around the world
Will not always get it done
but being a decent human being
Raising a family daughters or sons

Everyone cannot be an actor
It's hard enough to play your role
We can treat each other with respect
That's a story your magic will hold

We can teach our kids about equity
Where everyone has a chance to learn
Respecting diversities of cultural
Then fairness is everywhere you turn

Policeman, Fireman, Doctor or Lawyer
Go ahead, pull a rabbit out of a hat
You always have a chance to choose
if you believe nothing else in life believe that

God gave us a certain magic
That no one else can perceive
If you fail to choose to be you
Then not even you will be pleased

Softer times

Ssofter times or times when
your kids won't for nothing at all
if they're not taught the no's of Life
At some point they will fall

My mom put food on the table
After cleaning some else's home
If she did this for other people
I make sure I take of my own

I only saw her cry one time
And she cried because of me
I felt worthless I caused my mom stress
That was not the son I wanted to be

I was just too young to understand
How my mom took care of her kids
Now that I am older I tip my hat
And raise children the way mom did

I never saw her pray at night
I guess because we were in bed
But I heard her sing quite often
Now I know her spirit was fed

Sometime she cooked and would sing
And take little bites here and there
She made sure that we were fed
Now I appreciate how much mom cared

The smell of bacon would wake us up
In the mornings before school
Yeah we got whipping time to time
Prayer was mom's most valuable tool

She has been gone since 1997
And I still miss her to this day
She made sure we knew our God
To show appreciation to God I pray

Acceptable

They call the American dream
Dreams where one can achieve
Depending on the color of skin
Nightmares are what we receive

From the military to Michael Jackson
White was all we could see
So they tried to make us think
That white is what we had to be

To live the life seen on TV
Come home to a family that loves you
Tell dad about common problems
Then solve them, that's what I do.

Little did I know it was for show
These lives lived on a TV
Called the N word and other names
Black is what I was proud to be

I was better than my white peers
More than 90% of the time
They couldn't beat or outsmart me
Paperwork and lies was all they could find

Michael wasn't so lucky
The media got ahold of his head
I think he felt if he wasn't white
Then he may as well be dead

Not that anyone ever told him
But media perception is for real
He tried and hoped to be accepted
But that just wasn't the deal

Everyone had their hand out
As if he owed them anything
All he wanted to do was be happy
Create his music, dance, and sing

When his talents were not enough
He tried to change his face
He did not have a clue
The black could not be erased

I wonder if he died not knowing
His original black would be tough
As a Black man living in America
Dreams will never be enough

The Power of Prayer

Through the power of Prayer
Samson fought for hours
with the Jawbone of an ass
Philistines were devoured

Through the power of Prayer
Jonah slept inside of a whale
He reached his final destination
without a boat or sail

Through the power of Prayer
The Battle of Jericho Was Won
Joshua played his horn all day
Under God's gift of the sun

Through the power of Prayer
Jesus fed a multitude
Five fish and two loaves of bread
Falling asleep was their gratitude

Through the power of Prayer
Our Ancestors were set free
Our fathers, fathers had no problem
When it came to bending at the knee

Through the power of Prayer
My wife and I would wed
At night we are able to laugh and talk
Before we rest our head

Through the power of Prayer
I am able to wake up every day
Helping to improve another's life
As God guides me on my way

The power of prayer proves itself
Time and time again
I am a testimony of prayer
Pray for yourself,, don't forget the Amen

Heaven's Lighthouse

When we lose our way in life
Guidance is what we seek.
We wave our hand to understand.
And the sky is where we speak

When we tend to lose a loved one
We know that God is there?
His reasons are his reasons.
Only God chooses to share.

Work all week to make ends meet.
Until the bills are all paid
We must move our feet if we are to eat
Through work efforts God has made

We often know when somethings wrong.
It is that feeling in our gut.
When it is time, a light will shine
Revealing answers to our what's

When the storms cover the skies
The wind the hail and rain
A rainbow shows to let us know.
That Jesus is still his name.

TIME 4 HEALING (MAKE IT MAKE SENSE)

Heaven is that light house light.
And the bible our GPS
Sometimes at night we lose sight.
Hoping the answer to prayers is yes.

You can give someone directions.
And suggest a way to go.
If they take time the GPS will find
Home is what it will show.

We Gone Let It shine

When I look at other people
And the problems they go through.
I know our love is not perfect.
But I would rather do it with you

Things are going to take work.
Marriage will take time.
We will not get it right day and night
If we do not understand that is fine

We share what is bothering us
So that we may understand
How to be a better husband and wife
A better woman a better man

We have experienced so many things.
Sharing our dreams
When people love and trust each other
They can do anything it seems

I Love and trust this woman.
To thee I the wed
We could have had anyone.
But we chose each other instead.

TIME 4 HEALING (MAKE IT MAKE SENSE)

I do not think we have forgotten.
The reasons why we are here.
Our hearts want the same things.
Which from the start was clear?

Our communication is descent.
But it is not completely at its best.
It may not be the best in the world.
Our life, our love, our test

Strong Who

The strength to be you
Has to come from within
Better to build a strong child
Then to mend broken Men

The world will try to defeat you
Afraid of your strength
They can only see halfway
While you go to full length

They will plant bugs
and they will plant seeds
Trying to find your weakness
So they can succeed

Do not look over your shoulder
But You must watch out
God will fight your battles
That is what he is about

It is hard to walk that road
Temptation a trail of plenty
Night and day you must pray
Standing for the hearts of many

TIME 4 HEALING (MAKE IT MAKE SENSE)

Season in and season out
Black men under attack
Buttons pushed in due time
The right thing is no act

Remember That Story

Every now and then a story
Will touch the bottom of your heart
In an incredibly unique way
Listening to it makes you a part

Your feel the feels that make it real
Compassion touches your soul.
A story filled with certain emotions.
Each time the story is told.

You try not to cry then you sigh.
But the tears roll any ole way
Inspired by an inner strength.
Is how you make it through the day

We all have a certain story.
That makes us rise to our feet.
Search for answers on the inside
Not knowing about a defeat

You stick with it never to quit
Though times may become trials
Deep down inside you try to hide
Forcing frowns into smiles

No one can tell your story.
Or see it the way that you do
Dreamed your dream's so it seems.
Happy conclusions, depend on you.

You may pray for another day.
God is the editor of your story.
In the end see where it began
Who deserves all the glory?

The Magic of Love

I've embraced the lips of women
But none quite like this
A pleasure that was so erotic
It all transpired from a kiss

A sweet smell of cinnamon
To sensualize the event
Sex never presented itself
But when she came I went

I looked into her eyes
She passionately stirred back
Kissing her eyes rubbing her thighs
Her trembling was not an act

I placed my hand carefully
To massage her inner esteem
Her breath captivated my senses
We begin to create a dream

The more that we kissed
The warmer the atmosphere became
A time that wasn't meant to be
We both knew and felt the same

TIME 4 HEALING (MAKE IT MAKE SENSE)

I wasn't about to let go
I could tell neither was she
It may not have been our time
But this time was going to be

A place my hand inside her love
Is she slowly parted her thighs
As we began to slowly make love
She held on and closed her eyes

When I came then she came
Then we both came out loud
Every breath became her last
As she would breathe aloud

Ear to ear we would cheer
An indulging plight of ecstasy
We had both just made love
Capturing the meaning of intimacy

A moment filled with magic
And like magic it all disappeared
A commemorative one-time event
A moment that would be revered

Chapter Three

Smell the Healing

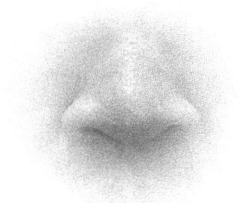

When a fart is a fart

A fart is not a fart
Unless it makes your nose turn

A fart is a fart
If it can make buttermilk churn

A fart so stinky
It can make you take a bow

A fart so strong
You wonder where it came from and how

A fart is a fart
Is when it leaves a green mist

A fart left silent
And people are left pissed

A smell so strong
You think the funky of a skunk

A fart so nasty
It didn't stink, it stunk

A fart is a fart
If it stinks up a good suit

If it is not this strong,
Then your fart was just a poot

Adam and Eve (The Fall of Paradise) The Alternate Ending

Look at the story of Adam and Eve
And how it all began.
How eve ate that apple
Was she enticed by man or woman?

The ancient watered-down version
Really does not tell it all.
About the surmise of paradise
And how Adam & Eve came to fall.

We all know the story.
Of how the serpent showed his face
He talked to eve and rapped to eve
To make her bow in disgrace

The devil slithered to Eve
He attracted her with a kiss.
Told her things she wanted to hear.
Until she became remised

Why is Adam always working?
He is always hanging around God
He needs to pay more attention to you.
If you were mine, you would be my job

The Eve would nod her head?
As if she were to agree.
He convinced her to eat the apple.
And that's how sin came to be.

When she ate the apple
Poor Adam was soon to follow.
When he ate that apple
Sin was tough yet easy to swallow

Then when God appeared to them
He asked why do you hide?
Presenting to him their nakedness
Ashamed where is your pride.

Adam blamed it all on Eve.
That is when the trend began.
Passing blame to someone else
Instead of standing up as a man

Why do we seem so surprised now?
Satan did it way-back then
He gives us things we think we want.
Again, and again, and again

If we think of our time now
And how it was long ago.
Did we learn from Adam and Eve?
This life is what we must show.

If you think the devil does not exist
Why don't you just ask Eve?
Just look at the road you travel.
You should have a reason to believe.

Inspired by Sophia Farrar

My United States Air Force

I fought for a country
that didn't fight for me
no one seem to care
is this how it should be

With the George Floyd incident
my eyes sought to see
that there were other people
who felt just like me

Sitting on painful incidents
after all these years
Various miffs arose
Still fighting back the tears

Memories would rewind
Just like a video tape
Back then we all took
More than a man should take

To see some white Airmen
get away with their crimes
when if I'm 2 minutes late
my life stopped on a dime

Padding assessment paperwork
So whites could make rank
While Airmen who did the work
Who didn't fly would sank.

With all the experiences shared
And all the people met
I am thankful for the man I am
Times I never will forget

Through the grace of a God
Who was watching over me
Guiding my steps while I slept
To be the man I needed to be

The Privilege of Waking Up

There have been a couple of nights
That my chest took a beating
God showed his mercy on me
And woke me with his greeting

Blue skies the sun came out
And still I could open my eyes
I was still on God's wake up list
To my life it was my surprise

Nights when I couldn't breathe
But I pushed out the wind
God is also a forgiving God
He died for all of us and our sins

I wouldn't have seen 63 years
If God hadn't made a way
I know that we're blessed
it is why we pray every day

I try not to complain
But sometimes it's a shame
How people go through life
And never speak his name

They woke up all by themselves
That God had no say
Then when they get in trouble
They turn to him and pray

You don't pray after the trouble
You pray before it begins
Giving thanks to God
Who provides support within.

Country Skies

Depending on where you stand
Skies have a different view
Feelings have a different meaning
Different for me, different for you

If on the ground in St Ives
With history in its past
Mince meat pies served with fries
When famished won't last

If on the ground In Amsterdam
The sky is filled with stitch
Then the nose becomes exposed
The face won't give an inch

The London skies and it's rise
An experienced to be had
To know that lies fill the skies
Sowed by mom's and dad's

Then on the ground in Texas
Looking out over this land
Blessed to be this land and me
In God is where we stand

Even though lies feel some skies
The truth is what you should see
In the end from where it began
Is where our lives will be

Little Stinker

Stepped into the restroom.
Just to take a leak
The stench was so foul.
It was in my clothes for a week.

You could tell from the smell.
He was the man in his house.
This smell was so strong.
That it would choke a mouse

Suddenly the toilet rang out.
As the water rushed to the lid
Out from the stall he was small.
Stepped this 7-year-old kid.

Are you going to be, okay?
Was the question I asked?
The smell was so bad.
I thought I needed a mask.

The he just smiled and sighed.
Man, that felt good.
Knee high to a water bucket
Was how tall he stood.

How could something so foul?
Come from something so small.
That was the smell from a man.
Two hundred pounds six'6' inches tall

Then as he left the bathroom
All I could do was shake my head.
There could only be one conclusion.
Something inside of him was dead.

Names on God's List

Today I was on God's list.
I was able to get out of bed.
Since I was on that list
I woke up and bowed my head.

Giving thanks for another day
This day I opened my eyes
Embracing moments in the day
Earth complimented the skies.

Today I was on God's list.
Taking in a breath to breathe
Knowing that it is up to me.
God's word well received.

If there should come a day
My name is not on God's list.
May the cold of my soul?
Warm family when missed.

When that song comes on
Jokes told over, and over again.
May the sense of hearing?
Bring them a healing, Amen!

When they think of my smile
And the laugh soon to follow.
Let their tears erase their fears.
Their spirit no longer wallows.

Reading the poems in my book
Let them bring peace of mind
Will Alice Mack and Aunt Pearl
Be on that list next to mine

God has a list of names
Of whom will and will not wake?
All our names are on this list.
Who will have our souls to take?

Chose to Learn

Everyone has a choice to choose.
So which choice do you chose?
Is the choice for all within your call?
Or just the one in your use.

You should never burn a bridge.
Where there is a barrage of traffic
Bridges burned and nothing learned.
No one sees you even when sick.

There is always a choice to choose.
One is best the other better.
In your mind you must find
Christ; get your thoughts together.

Mom and dad's time will pass.
Now the ears will yield.
At times you did not want to hear it
God picks flowers from his field.

You must now face life head on
No phone call to save the day.
In the rough when things were tough
God use his flowers to pave the way.

You make a choice good or bad.
And live with your result.
Time will fly as your kids rely.
On you to now be God's consult

Everyone has a choice to choose.
In God, the choice is always blessed.
In your heart choice is the part
Where you always give your best

Down Low

Most reach that pinnacle
Where it is time to retire
Should I stay or should I go?
Apply for a new rehire.

Everyone has a plan in place.
Reaching lifetime milestone's
The only regret to be met.
Are friends who moved on?

Parents have moved on.
New patriarch, matriarch bound.
Guidance is a whole new order.
Traditions to be sought and found.

Longevity can be a good thing.
But not if you are all alone.
Because of God's amazing grace
Friends and enemies are gone.

Not to be harsh but this is fact.
God redirects people and paths.
If you should find in your mind
You are standing alone in aftermath.

Those who left tend to leave.
With no thought left in sight
People leave we cannot conceive.
Making it hard to sleep at night

So, if you happen to find.
You are the only one left in time
The down low is a definite go.
All of you share a piece of mind.

Through The Eyes of Hate

I've tried to imagine the other side
But it's hard for me to do
Hating for no reason at all
I just can't see that me in you

I always look over my shoulder
And I've tried my best not to
In all my life the hate and strife
Won't look past the evil you do

The people who I try to imagine
Or are young white kids today
If they were not taught to hate
Is there solace to come your way

It is hard for me to try and see
A world of hate through your eyes
You chose to kill, no mercy at will
What kind of days feel your skies

I Imagine God's hands are full
Choices between right and wrong
We all have to rise and wake
To days for some that seem long

I close my eyes to my surprise
I try to see what you see
The kind of hate your mind creates
Is a person that I chose not to be

I am thankful for a God
Who places my name on a list
To rise and shine a day enshrined
With events that some will miss

The Smell of Healing

Have you ever been driving in a car
and thinking about your day
A smell suddenly crosses your nose
To take your breath away

A time locked inside your mind
Smiles implode the face
Mind travel is at its best
Taking you a certain time and place

Homemade German chocolate cake
Bacon to make you wake
Deep in sleep the smell creeps
That smell is all it takes

From the smell of morning dew
To a women's sweet perfume
Reminds you of a romance
The heart and mind is consumed

Then the feeling that you felt
When sharing a moments together
Controls a nose that will not close
That won't let you forget her

Then in your mind you try to find
why it all had to end
Would you do it all over
If you had it to do over again

Apple, pecan, sweet potato pies
Sends delight to the smell
Holidays and special days
Is a scent that every story tells

You can tell from a certain smell
What kind of day it will be
The sense of smell a healing smell
Does it every time for me

God gave us the memories
And the smells that we embrace.
That come from out of nowhere
Leaving that happy on our face

That Last Breath

The last breath is a countdown
To how life has run its toll
Reminiscing about the things
That life used to behold

Watching a person get old
After living all this time
All the laughter all the tears
Are things that come to mind

You never really think about life
Until life is in your face
There are certain memories
That you just cannot replace

You remember the advice
All the fun and games
When that last breath hits
Nothing else will be the same

All you can do for you
Is to take the best from it all
Remember what it's like to stand
During the times you fall

Let the lessons learned
Be the guide in your light
Then maybe, just maybe
You will get this life thing right

The Smell of Hickory

Riding home from work one night
volleyball was the game
A Hickory smell brushed my nose
and the ride just was not the same

I was taken a-back
To a peaceful place and time
With the prevalence of evil
Absent from the front of mind

The ride was filled with thoughts
As headlights revealed the dark
All I could see were good times
My history made his mark

Then the truck came to a stop
The memories continued to roll
Racing barefoot in the street
Against the young and old

My grandfather whipped us all
Laughing as he won
We took that whipping that day
Our grandfather wasn't done

He barbecued and told stories
About being a younger man
Running through fields of chucker bugs
Hustling to save his land.

Then someone honked their horn
Prompting me to go
The lights came on the memory gone
That was the end of the show.

Chapter Four

Taste the Healing

A Little Taste of Home

Have you ever had a taste of joy
To make your whole face shine
Like the pit from a peach seed
To the bottom of a watermelon rind

We would butter our toast
With some lightly scrambled eggs
No matter what my mother would eat
My siblings and I would beg

We would have crackers and fish
That came in that little silver can
Then mom would make salmon croquet
So good we ate it with our hands

Ooooh, mom would make our favorite
Red beans with ground up meat
Hot water corn bread on the side
Then freeze some for later to eat

All of our clothes were school clothes
No matter what we had
With food to eat a place to sleep
Blessed, even when times were sad

TIME 4 HEALING (MAKE IT MAKE SENSE)

Sometimes we get caught up
About how God brought us so far
If we sit back then just like that
We would see who we truly are

I Will Never Smile That Way Again

A funny thing about mom
She could always make us smile
Things she said and things she did
Made it fun being a child

Even though clothes were cheap
We were always dress up neat
During the task we never asked
Our clothes were ours to keep

There were times I made her say
But she'd never she had a tear
She always remained strong for us
And never showed signs of fear

Mom died on a Monday
And we buried her 5 days later
Mom and I were best of friends
Recollections of fun filled laughter

I stopped beside her grave site
To visit my mom one day
There was no special reason
I wanted to sit where she lay

TIME 4 HEALING (MAKE IT MAKE SENSE)

I missed the late night phone calls
And those holiday hello's
I know that mom is painless
God said Alice it's time to go

Just to hear her voice on the phone
The smiles that it would bring
Mom and I talked about everything
But never discussed anything

These are days I leave behind
For I take with me the good
Mom lay rest in peace
I now stand where you stood

My mother is gone forever
For I've lost my very best friend
Now whenever I answer the phone
I know I'll never smile that way again

Eat to Live don't Live to Eat

Poor little fat girl
Eating everything in sight
Poor little fat girl
Cannot sleep at night

Poor little fat girl
Caught up in her sleep
Poor little fat girl
Someone cared to peep

Poor little fat girl
Life taken at a glance
Poor little fat girl
Will you get another chance

Poor little fat girl
Take care of yourself
Poor little fat girl
Destiny is all you have left

Poor little fat girl
Push away the food
Poor little fat girl
Your rude is there rude

Take a look at that girl
Walking around with a grin
Take a look at that girl
People are starring again

Take a look at that girl
All buffed up and proud
Take a look at that girl
Her quiet speaks out loud

Take a look at that girl
Selective with her chow
Take a look at that girl
Just look at you now

The Favor to Savor

When you are in a parent's favor
They will do anything for you.
Wash your clothes and clean your room.
And search for your lost shoe

They will cook your favorite meal.
All you need to do is ask.
Because you are their favorite child
It is a pleasure instead of a task.

They brag about you to their friends.
The pride just rolls right in
If they could have another child
They would do you all over again

Christmas time is really Christmas.
Santa Clause, lives with you
There is no naughty because of nice
The Easter bunny likes you to.

Oh, but never let that favor end.
Now everyone is upset.
It is no longer what you deserve.
You deserve what you get.

The curfew no longer extended.
Be in this house, be on time.
If you are even one minute late
Son your butt is mine

They never come to your events.
Be it on and off the court.
You never savor losing favor.
Due to a lack of support

So, with this glance take this chance.
To make your parents proud
Find that favor that you can savor.
A parent pride can be loud.

Easter Who

Easter is a time that we celebrate
The resurrection of Jesus Christ
A man who delivered us from our sins
Not only once but twice

He washed the eyes of the blind
Made it possible for them to see
He told all who could hear his call
To see my kingdom believe in me

Feeding the hungry and touching the lame
Who could suddenly get up and walk
He snatched the demon from an angry man
And now the mute can talk

A boat be-stilled from his disciples ills
With the muttering of a few words
Soon all found out of miracles spread about
From the tips of tongues people heard

He spoke to his followers in parables
And they would listen, all were quiet
He closed the mouth of an angry lion
Now suddenly the lion is on diet

He pulled a man from the belly of a whale
And walked on waters of lakes
All you have to do is believe
A little faith is all it takes

He's a map for those who lost their way
The mornings that we call good
In the past I have come to know his name
If you don't then maybe you should

That Turkey on Thanksgiving

Turkey on Thanksgiving has meaning.
And how it is all cut up.
Mom no longer ate dinner with a fork.
She had to sip it from a cup.

Her body stopped doing the things.
That it used to do
That was hard for me to accept.
It would be that way for you to

She was the type of mother.
Where everything must be-done
The day before the day of grace
Our house was always the one.

People would stop by and chat
Blessing us with their words
To tell about how life was going
There were so many stories heard.

Talking about how life took turns
Turns for good and turns for bad.
On those good ole turkey days
Times would be happy and be sad.

Thanksgiving memories I now have.
Meaning we managed to make.
Built on the concept of mom.
Reminiscent of magic she baked.

Pies, cakes, puddings, and cobbler
Dressing and Turkey's to boot
A household filled with smell goods.
At days end, we sleep, and we toot

Building tradition for my sons
Is especially important to see.
I know one day I will be gone.
I showed them what Thanksgiving should be.

Quit It

Anyone can roll over.
But you do not have to die.
Do whatever you need to do!
But get up after you cry.

People who depend on you
Watch you when you roll!
If you do it too often
Then the rolling gets old

How can they depend on you?
When you cannot stand
How does your daughter choose?
A husband for a man

How is your oldest son?
Expected to lead a household?
When you had a chance to stand
But you chose to roll.

Let us not forget the wife!
Who on your shoulders fall?
Sought and later caught.
By a man strong enough to stand tall

Her man failed to rise in her eyes.
And lead their family and kids.
If she had the vision to see the future
She could do more than he did

The Inside Man

Having all the talent in the world
Will not get you across the line.
From childhood to adulthood
Thick is what you will find.

Having every excuse to fail
Using it as a crutch
Anyone would die for talent.
You happen to have that touch.

Feeling sorry for yourself
Choosing to lay pride aside
If coaches chose to dig deep
They may find some heart inside

No one can take you by the hand.
To guide you along the way
Eventually you will wake up.
But what will you see that day?

Will you see the life you have?
Vs what it could have been.
You wish you had it to do over
So, you do not end up here again

TIME 4 HEALING (MAKE IT MAKE SENSE)

Wiping away the go-between
Trapped in all those years.
How you choose to win or lose
Is found between your ears.

Constantly in a struggle
You must make it through somehow
Finding a way to succeed
There is no time like now

This Crazy Life

Crazy as a bed bug
Crazy as can be
Crazy like their mother
Crazy just like me

Just plain crazy
For no reason at all
Crazy how they stand
Crazy how they fall

Crazy how they look
Crazy how they see
Crazy just to be crazy
Humbling how crazy can be

Crazy sense of keen
Crazy with mad skills
Crazy how they are healthy
Crazy quick to fall ill

Crazy not to help
Crazy not to care
Crazy the hand out
Crazy want to share

Crazy the advice
Crazy they don't hear
Crazy is the face
Shedding a crazy tear

Crazy how they live
Crazy not to pray
Crazy how they see God
It is just crazy either way

Crazy not to love
Crazy how we hate
Crazy with no remorse
Crazy will be fate

Crazy the pain
Crazy the ordeal
Crazy the trust
Crazy the reveal

Crazy all these things
Crazy, nothing to say
Crazy you will look back
Crazy with be that day

Life will Happen

As life happens to us all
Our thoughts become much deeper.
Commemorating moments in life
Because lessons do not get cheaper

The first thing that happens
You analyze the situation.
Unaware of its outcome
You experience a new sensation.

Life love and happiness
Will hit each of us in stages.
First marriage first divorce
Love, our emotional wages

Hampered by life experiences.
It is difficult to expound.
You find yourself in situations.
That have yet to be found.

Chalk the lessons in your belt.
The next time they arise.
So now the next time you see it
It should come as no surprise.

Life will happen to us all.
Open our mind and thoughts.
Time becomes expensive.
With the lessons that are taught

Shrinage

It was an early Monday morning.
Taking her car to the shop
There was a stain of constant rain.
It did not seem like it would stop.

Taking in a Quacker Barrell
Just to grab something to eat
Starring from across the table
The company could not be beat.

We sat talking about anything.
No subject was off the table.
We laughed the entire time.
With God's grace we were able

The phones were there?
But then they were not there
Appearing was the presence of love.
We could feel it in the Air.

We drove back to our home.
To await the mechanic's call
Driving that way made the day.
Radio songs would say it all.

Today was a memory created?
Touching the back of minds
We could live our lives this way.
Our love, our life, our shrine

Chapter Five
The Sound of Healing

Princess Sophia and Earl's Girl

Once there was a fairytale Princess
Sophia was her name.
She was drop dead beautiful.
Her smile was her claim to fame.

    All the villagers loved her.
    And would always stop to visit.
    She had a heart made of gold.
    And her disposition was exquisite.

She was in love with a prince.
Who would offer her the world?
Not because she was a Princess.
For she was the girl of Earl

    They had magical moments together.
    Blessed by the hand of God.
    They could do most anything.
    Activities would never seem odd.

They could sit and watch paint dry
And talk about their day.
She would talk and he would listen.
Pretending not to hear what she would say.

She would get upset.
And claim he needs to pay attention.
Prince Earl would truly play his role.
Until there was something to mention

They would soon marry.
And take each other's hand.
Do you Earl take this woman?
And Sophia takes this man.

To have and to hold
Until the days you grow old
Sophia will do what is asked.
And Earl just does what he is told.

Her ring was presented.
You may now kiss the bride.
Even though they had their happy
They were both grateful inside.

Love until now would elude them.
In relationships they had before
Since man did not create this union
They would seek to love no more.

In God's House

I found myself worshiping God
In a well-used house of prayer
When the doors finally open
People were sweating everywhere

I had to find a place to stand
For it was standing room only
The choir singing a joyful noise
As well as the woman next to me

Feet tapping hands a clapping
With pianos organs and tambourines
People were shouting in the aisles
While others rocked and screamed

I went to use the restroom
And the toilet leaned to one side
Then I noticed the whole church leaned
Even with everyone inside

You think with all that rejoicing
This church would give way and fall
That wouldn't happen this day
Because God was holding us all

I also noticed people were dressed
With nice suits and Levi-Strauss
I had always heard of places like this
I was standing in God's house

Silent Strength

There is a certain strength
Common to us all
Muscles brawn and biceps
Strong is what it is called

Then there's a survivor's will
That shows a different strength
It is the power of endurance
Which is evident in its limit

There is an emotional strength
That must come from within
A strength that must succeed
Time and time Again

There is a strength we know
That is witnessed by us all
A strength that is apparent
But very seldom recalled

This is the strength of a mother
Mothers have to be strong
She must care and show love
Whether she is right or wrong

Passionate is she in statue
Yet disciplined is her hand
A silent strength unknown to all
Only moms can understand

Displaying unconditional love
Until there is nothing left
A silent strength that must abide
When anger must regulate itself

She takes no credit when right
Just to accommodate the wrong
Modest was she until the end
When she was right all alone

That Old Couch

My wife and I bought a couch
It had seen it's better days
When you squat to take a seat
Comfort leaves you amazed

It was old and dilapidated
Coming apart at the seams
Whomever laid down to sleep
Knew it could create dreams

It was Gray made of twill
Throw pillows on the back
Couch covered throw blankets
Stained memories of snacks

We could afford a new one
But this one felt so darn good
When it was time to watch movies
Assigned seats were understood

We finally bought a new couch
And put the old one outside
There it set in the shed
A lifetime of secrets inside

One day I arrived home
Wife nowhere to be found
Looking upstairs calling her name
She was nowhere around

Outside asleep on the couch
She was peaceful not a sound
Sleeping as if she owned the couch
It was like an angel laid her down

That old couch was like a friend
Supporting our family for years
The couch does what couches do
With movies the smiles the tears

Candid Conversations

Candid conversations
Our conversations to be had
Transparency is the key
No matter how good or bad

Things are put on the table
Everyone becomes aware
Of expectations to survive
No matter when or where

When conversations can't be had
Lies become the truth
It's bad when you find it out
Worse when it steals your youth

Some twist conversation
A trying to make you believe
To make their lie your truth
When the intent is to deceive

It's hard to be candid
When you have things to hide
Those who float the lies you note
Are only there for the ride

Continuing to hide what's inside
When you know it is a lie
One day come out leaving to pout
Tell the truth before you die

Mama Knew Something

Mama use the same things
That I really didn't understand
Things I would realize later
But not until I was a man

Girls and I were an item
We'd See each other every day
Mama said take your time
You wear out welcome that way

Then I wanted to do things
Because everybody else did
Mama said be your own man
Even though I was still a kid

Then I moved from mama's house
And thought no more rules
Little did I know about life
Mama said you have tendencies of a mule

I took women home to meet my mom
She would say she's not right for you
I thought to myself mama don't know
Nobody makes me feel like you do boo

With Sheila money ran short
And rent was always due
Bills began to stack up
Time with Sheila did to

Finally I couldn't take anymore
I asked mama what should I do
Before finishing my sentence
Mama said baby, mama already knew

She said son you have to be patient
But relief was nowhere in sight
Mama came to the rescue
She never said once she was right

She held me in her arms
And put her hand on my head
Everything is going to be all right
Mama knows, because God said

That thing you do

There is that little thing you do.
That seems to make me smile.
Like when you say something clever
That affords you so many guilds.

When you laugh from the heart
The room just seems to shine
A feeling that feels so amazing
You know that things will be fine.

The way you smack your lips.
When you know you are right
How you tend to express yourself
Every day and every night

How you tend to see the world
Wisdom as smart as a street
People know and respect you.
Because they know your heartbeat

Then there is a certain way
You tend to make me feel
That way that only you can do.
Giving our lives an appeal

You do have those that will try.
To corrupt that thing that you do
People who tend to be jealous
Because of the you that you do

TIME 4 HEALING (MAKE IT MAKE SENSE)

Some People

Some people enter your life
only to deceive
when they get what you've got
it's time for to leave

Playing the game its ashamed
Pretending to be friends
The road gets tough life is rough
Crashing in the end

They eat your food man how rude
and even spend the night
All along their plan is to wrong
Out of mind out of sight

Laugh at your jokes you are not woke
They can see the sleep in your eyes
Having your trust which is a must
The rest will end in cries

They sleep with your wife that is life
Then pretend everything is all good
If she is weak she will not speak
Because they know where you stood

TIME 4 HEALING (MAKE IT MAKE SENSE)

Now you have to throw it away
Their expiration ended that day
All you can do is walk away
There is nothing in life left to say

Beware of your inner circle
and where the hands connect
Held together by fingertips
Will lead to self and disrespect

What used to be taboo
Has now become the ooh
Leaving one to shake their head
Wow! is that what they do?

Maintain strength at any length
because that is not the end
God gave it once he will give twice
Prayer will start your life again

When we Fellowshipped

People may not remember this.
Because it did not relate to them
How church members would gather
Saturday nights just to sang hymns.

Folks used to fellowship.
Holidays never spent along.
They would gather around for sound.
Celebrating the season with songs

Violet Morris, Mitchel, and others
Played piano's singing in praise.
Nights filled with hallelujahs.
Amen, this is how we were-raised.

Sundays would be a carryover.
From the Saturday night before
Hot chocolate juice and cookies
Then praise would hit the floor

The pastor would stop by
And there was always a spread
The food was just one treat.
The other treat, breaking bread

A house filled with the spirit.
Satan was nowhere around.
Not one eye would remain dry.
The holy spirit blessing sounds

The more they would shout
The more they would sing.
Just to be in the room
Was truly an inspiring thing.

God stopped by now and then.
Blessing souls, hearts, and minds
It is how we used to fellowship.
Man, I sure miss those times.

Dedicated to Greater New Friendship Baptist Church Pastor G.T. Thomas

Magical Moments

There are moments filled with magic
when happiness touches your face.
The sun shines at certain times
You know it is through God's grace.

There's a tingle in your feet.
Prompting you to want to dance.
Make a choice to use your voice
Choosing positive circumstance.

Your kids show their upbringing
As only you know they would
The chest of a proud parent
Pride stands where you stood

Then the magic hits the fan
Whenever any child is born
Teaching them right from wrong
At times choices leave you torn.

Magical moments when you win
All the arduous work paid off
At times you had to be tough
and still your heart remains soft.

There in bed you lay your head
And close your eyes to sleep
Next day you wake, and you pray
Thank you! yesterday was sweet.

Speaking for a Friend

Some people enter your life
only to deceive
when they get what you've got
It is time for them to leave

Playing a game, it is a shame
Pretending to be friends
The road is tough, life is rough
Crashing in the end

Eating your food man how rude
Under your roof spend the night
All along their plan is to wrong
For real friends that is not right

Laugh at your jokes you are not woke
They can see the sleep in your eyes
Having your trust which is a must
The rest will come in cries

Sleeping with your wife that is life
Then pretend everything is all Goode
If she is weak she will not speak
By August you know where you stood

Now you have to throw it away
Their expiration ended that day
All you can do is walk away to
There is nothing in life left to say

Beware of your inner circle
and where the hands connect
Held together by fingertips
Will lead to a gross disrespect

What used to be taboo
Has now become the ooh
Leaving those to shake heads
WOW! is that what they do?

Maintain strength at any length
Because that is not the end
God gave once he can give twice
When prayer starts life begins.

The Day You Became Who

It can take someone to see you.
To show you who you want to be.
Then you wonder where you have been
A true reflection is what you see.

Others will not like your transformation.
While others will embrace the real you
The people who really care about you
Will endorse the good you do.

You ask the question with each success.
Where has this person been?
You love the who that is now you
And wish you could do it sooner again

The only self-endorsement
Seen through the pain you bare
You no longer share your discontent.
You are the only one who cares.

Things you did for everyone else
You now begin to do for you.
As your circle become smaller
You can now see who is who?

People will leave while others fall off.
Either way they are gone
Is it better to be unsuccessful in crowds?
Than to stand happy while alone

A Family Thing

Family should instruct families.
What a family should really be
I saw it when I was a child
Let me share with you what I see

Family will get on your nerve.
Speaking a peace of mind
Paying no bills still they feel
They have a say at times.

I never saw my mom hit.
By a man living in our house
Till this day I live to say
I have never hit my spouse.

The struggle is real, they feel.
Trying to make ends meet.
Even when dead the gap spreads
Kids too lazy to find their feet

Until children take a place
To put in place a new old
Generation to generation
Poverty will continue to roll.

It does not have to be.
What we live what we see
God gave us a mind to think.
To be who we need to be.

Family will not let you see.
What God wants you to be?
Envy sticks his head in
It does not like what it sees.

Why should you do better?
We are both the same.
When they did not embrace God
And fail to know his name.

Family may call his name
But not know him at all
This is when the knees bend.
The family will hear him call

TIME 4 HEALING (MAKE IT MAKE SENSE)

The Time I Needed God

The time that I needed God.
I found a way to pray.
I will never do this again
If you help me out this day

I remember taking a ferry.
And the ship began to sway
I knew I could not swim.
So, to God I began to pray.

Take me through this storm.
I will never do this again.
After I prayed to God
My last word to him, Amen

A car crashed in front of me
Stopped at a light.
I did not have anywhere to go.
I must be living life right

I was asleep one night.
And my chest began to hurt.
God if it be your will.
May I stay on this side of the dirt?

My first marriage began to tank.
I fell to both of my knees.
God send someone for me.
A New Year's Eve prayer, PLEASE

My mom, dad, and auntie passed.
And the tears filled my eyes
I asked God to give me strength.
For my family he heard my cries

Leading family, the way we were lead.
God give me the strength to lead
That is why I write what I write
My poetry is what they read.

I found myself thanking God.
With every reason to pray
A light came on that is always on
I need God every day.

A Song of Healing

There can be a sound you hear.
That tugs on the strings of the heart.
Songs you hear time again.
That in you, it becomes a part.

No matter what the mood
It will always do the trick.
To lift your spirits no matter what
Whether angry, happy, or sick

It does something to the soul
Where the tears control you face
Songs humble the heart and mind.
Your head is in the right space.

"His Eye is on the Sparrow"
Reminds me of simpler times.
Reciting poems, and speeches
Christmas, Easter plays, and rhymes

Watching all the congregation
Clapping their hands with Amen
Smiles on the faces of everyone.
Then next year, doing it again.

I sang a song on children's day.
And my grandmother would attend.
"Where you going to run to?"
A song I sang back then.

Everyone was in their seat.
Rejoicing to the sound of my voice
Whenever I would hit a note
I could hear my grandmother's voice

My mom had a voice back then.
I think why, she was proud.
It was like the more she clapped.
I raised my voice to the clouds.

After church was over
There were cheers and pats on the back
Congrats from my grandmother.
"I didn't know you could sing like that."

They have reached the other side.
Smiling on us from above
Whenever I hear those songs
My heart feels nothing but love.

Christian Expectation

Christian expectations
Are how Christians are expected to act
Actions that have come in question
So let us all examine this facts

To live our lives accordingly
We should be forgiving to forget
Holding on to what imprisons you
Will allow you to live life with regrets

"How can you hate your fellow man
And love God who you cannot see"
He is the creator of all mankind
His light in us is who we should be

Raise children with a steady hand
They don't need you as a friend
They have enough of those in life
They need you to get them to the end

There is no cost to pack a smile
See your neighbor and then say hi
Don't let grudges of the world
Let you see them and pass them by

You should lend a helping hand
We have all fallen at one time
The expectation of a Christian
Is the make that man a friend of mine

We should lift each other up
instead of tearing each other down
Christians want everyone to win
For the love in Christ we are found

Adult to adult we should consult
On what is best for the world
This is the expectation of our God
As his Christian boys and girls

Happy Employment

Everyone lives a life of happiness
but some people live it in parts
Happiness should be full time
Turning on and off the heart

Happy comes to them in spurts
But angry is most of the time
They can't enjoy life to the fullest
The past is stuck in their mind

They find it difficult to let go
They know they were wrong
Now a life were nights are short
And the days seem oh so long

They master the smile of fake
To brush emotions to the side
Trying to present a happy facade
When its resentment they hide

Still they chose to rise and find
A reason to exist each day
Others are blessed to rise and shine
And let God lead their way

"Happy is as happy does"
If Forest's mom had something to say
People can chose to be happy
Or let anger and hate consume the day

Full time happy, part time happy
What is in your heart?
If you chose to pray before each day
God takes care of the other part

The Preovulation of GOD

Thinking you could break me
but that just wasn't the case
so here I am the man I am
right here in your face

Tried to downplay my efforts
Lifting someone else in lies
The flight of the white
Left you with the goodbyes

To see me for who I am
Your vision was never clear
Your hate would resonate
So, God delivered me here

Removing rubbish from my life
God replaced them with gems
Under his sun blessed with son's
I can see the me in them

Traveling a road carrying their load
Growing into their own man
Messages show as they grow
Leaning when they don't understand

Leaving them to their lives
I will not always be around
They will know before I go "I am proud"
Whenever my ashes are found

I leave you with this before I dismiss
Man does not determine fate
Against all odds go with God
Christian sisters and brother will relate

Things I Can See (May 10, 2022)

When Uncle Fletcher moves on
To be with all the rest
I will miss him too
Our lives were truly blessed

I can see them on high
looking down on me
Him telling them the things
They wish they could see

Smiling laughing shaking hands
With hugs saying Amen
He is just really excited
To see every one of them again

Some did not make it
To that side of the cloud
but that is still okay
Everyone else was still proud

Jasper is this, Jasper that
you guys would be proud
I see them preparing a place for me
my own personal cloud

They tell him "yeah we saw"
we kept filling up his cup
so he can continue to lead
Looking down is how they look up

They were all smiling
While nodding their heads
Watching Fletcher's excitement
Sharing how we were fed

He received his doctorate
Leadership in administration
The first doctor in the family
Creating a new destination

New goals and new highs
So that our family will strive
To show the grace of our God
While on Earth and still alive

I had diamonds fall from my crown
Yes I have made mistakes
Falling to pray I found my way
We have a God that never forsakes

Never let anyone take away
what you can do and achieve
because anything is possible
All you just believe

Pushing her way to the front
Mom would lead in song and prayer
Heavenly sounds came ringing down
Friends and other families were even there

God never said it would be easy
Christ carried his own cross
Own your own magic while here
And carry yours Like A Boss

Who Knew

Events take place in life
Living life on cruise control
Day in day out, night in night out
Routines eventually grow old

Life happens as life does
Changing the light of way
You discover a new in you
Now it's a brand new day

People began to take notice
Life takes a different road
Liking the person you become
Since born you were ode

Each day now has new meaning
You sleep then you awake
A different walk a different talk
The difference new life makes

The people in your circle
Begin to disappear
Who was there who is not
Actions make it clear

It feels so good to be new
The old is dead and gone
You deserve a new nerve
A heart with a new home

Who knew you would be you
Doing the things you do
Trust this day if I must say
God is the one who knew

Who Has You

A hard core exterior
Like that of a turtle shell
Deep inside his heart his mine
Is going through a living hell

He holds back the tears
That fight to come out
No one knows this man's woes
What black men are all about

Emotions always on parade
With decisions on display
We take a few moments alone
To wind down from the day

No fuss no fight
From darkness must come light
Always under judgment
Is he wrong or is he right

Remain strong the world looks on
You always bring it home
Your piece of mine their peace of mine
Real men built to the bone

TIME 4 HEALING (MAKE IT MAKE SENSE)

In his car or in his bed
The man cave or tool shed
Men who stress from a mess
Remain strong until dead

Giving up is around the corner
With yield nowhere in sight
We go through what you see in you
At any minute any man's fight

You are the glue they see in you
Where appreciation is not found
A presence of power hour by hour
Without sight without a sound

Know we see you trying to be you
In everything you say and do
God has you no matter what you do
From the outside who has you

Ultimate Loss

The devastation of loss
Can be too much to bear
Thinking of the one's we love
Soon are no longer there

Your mind your eyes your soul
Suddenly takes a hit
For one to know and lose that glow
This time that life is it

The face paves a road
For our tears to travel
All emotions in one place
Curled up to unravel

Everything seems to hurt
Silence becomes your friend
This day not too long ago
The beginning; the end

Then on that day
The spirit slips away
Wells of eyes fill the skies
In your heart your mind you pray

TIME 4 HEALING (MAKE IT MAKE SENSE)

Loss of friends reach an end
Everyone around you pains
The tears will dry from the eye
Memories; all that remains

Tributes are made
The loss of life is paid
Faith in God remains
In this life God has made

The Other Side of Happiness

The other side of happiness
Often held in high esteem
The kind of happiness that happens
Only in someone's dreams

You dream of waking up
In the arms of someone you love
Then all do out the day
They are all you can think of

You take walks in the park
Is holding hands while you smile
Time passes by without notice
Finding you've walked for miles

You eat at your favorite restaurants
Smiling over candlelight
You smile you kiss and you toast
The best part of the night

You look into each other's eyes
And you can see tomorrow
Knowing if you could feel their pain
You would suffer all their sorrows

TIME 4 HEALING (MAKE IT MAKE SENSE)

A movie, fireplace, and popcorn
Fall asleep and each other's arms
You awake from movie residue
Basting from each other's charms

The other side of happiness
Can be just an eye blink away
To find someone you truly love
Now that would be the day

Non-Believers

People have doubted God.
From the beginning on in
God has proven himself.
Time, and time again

He wakes us up daily.
Despite what we have done
Forgiving us one more time
In a day that has not begun

Taking us through the day
Through trials and life's events
God watching guiding our steps.
That's how his time is spent.

When our hearts are troubled
Unexpectedly he steps in
Removing, placing people in our lives
We can get it right once again.

Soon God will return.
Highlighting rights and wrongs
People will soon just disappear.
Not in death just gone.

TIME 4 HEALING (MAKE IT MAKE SENSE)

God will have his way.
Then peace will finally prevail
Living life, no lies no strife.
Doing right, not a hard sell

We have time to believe.
Forgiveness is not a demand.
On your knees ask God please
Help me see and understand.

A Father's Love

The love between a father and son
Can sometimes go unmentioned.
Grow to be a better man.
Is any father's true intention?

He knew what he went through.
For you to be a better you
So rough times between the lines
Is, what Pop wants you to do.

He teaches you to cut the grass.
Then pick up the leaves.
Teaches you how to count money.
So, no one can ever deceive.

Teaches you to drive a car.
So, you can depend on you.
If tears should ever crowd the eyes
It is what a good dad will do.

Teaching you to suck it up.
Life can sometimes be unfair.
Raise your head move forward instead.
No one else but you will care.

TIME 4 HEALING (MAKE IT MAKE SENSE)

He may not always say it.
But you know how he must feel.
Your dad will do things for you.
To tie a bond that seals

Then in the end despite the begin.
Your dad will teach you to pray.
Because our God against the odds
Will teach you to be a man one day.

Strength for the Strong

A man has a certain strength.
He must live with every day.
A strength he must endure alone.
Strength to find his own way.

No one else can walk in his shoes.
Or carry this man's load.
He must pick up and carry himself.
For to him his self he is ode

Some men are strong enough.
Leading his family in tough times
Knowing if his family is to rise.
His light will not always shine.

Some men are strong enough.
To parent when all alone
Because the wife he chose in life
Decided it is time to be gone.

Strong men will take a seed.
Not born from his own.
Raise that kid, lead that kid.
To grow and be strong

TIME 4 HEALING (MAKE IT MAKE SENSE)

What about the strength of missing
Guidance that provided a voice
No longer here, missed by tears.
Words that still provide a choice.

Where do the men of strength go?
When he lacks the will to be strong.
On knees he prays through those days
God had his back all along.

Storybook Dreams

We all have that dream
To marry our one and only
Sometimes it all works out
Sometimes it leaves you lonely

You dream the same dreams
Laugh the same laugh
Things seem to lineup
Because love is the math

Hard times hit you never quit
Together you are meant to be
People looking on the outside
We'll never see the love you see

Never feel the love you feel
Never sing the way you sing
The one and only hasn't arrived
To make that Queen and King

You hear about it in story books
A life bruised with tragedy
As life goes on you live on
In God you were meant to be

Some admire your strength
Others envy your Commitment
But they cannot live your lives
Even if they live in it

They don't have your heart
They don't have your mind
They don't see your dreams
Your storybook will win every time

The End

I was infuriated as an Educator

Thursday, Dec 16, 2021, was an eye opening and sad day for the academic community. Decency reared its beautiful head from an unlikely source, one of our students.

We had an incident during small group testing at the beginning of sixth period (10:00am). Two groups of students were taking their final exams and collaborating as per the instructions of the teachers of record in a small group setting as part of their accommodations.

During this small group environment, a box with 1-day old donuts (11) were sitting on the table in room 402. One of our students attending my high school who was small group testing with me asked if he could have a donut and was given permission to eat a donut. Donuts that were left over from a previous event the day before. The student who for the purpose of this incident we will call Student A was eating the donut he was given permission to indulge in. Student B also wanted a donut and used a paper towel to get a donut as well. When Student B got a donut one of the female educators in room 402 in building B yelled at the student who wanted a day-old donut that he could not have a donut and that he needed to put his donut back. Student B who was distraught did not understand why he could not have a donut when they were given permission to have a donut. I applaud Student B for complying to a very inappropriate demonstration of authority and simply replied after returning the donut to the box still wrapped in the paper towel that he used to get the donut. He simply stated, "You don't have to yell at me" Student A witnessing this gross abuse of authority tore half of his donut and shared it with Student B.

An administrator was asked to intervene in this incident without knowing all the facts and affording Due process to this situation before passing a judgement on the situation for using a small group room for small group testing that is used weekly for this sole purpose. The students were distracted by all the yelling stopped testing and addressed the situation and in all the students were asked to stop their testing after working for 20 minutes to move to the Building A Library to finish their testing. The students were so distraught that neither of the seven students scored higher than a forty on their final exam. If are to be in the business of doing what is best for the students, then let us do what is best for the students no matter the student, no matter their history.

We have all witnessed situations where one moment can change the lives of an individual forever. If you hate your job and will carry a grudge for a student who you no longer support, then education may not be the place for you. If you are here for the paycheck, then there are other places that will also pay you a fair wage and you do not have to carry a grudge against a 17- or 18-year-old student. Today an adult had to learn a lesson from a student about human decency. I hope you were paying attention.

Day of Decency
December 16, 2021

A kid gave a kid half of his donut.
Because his was taken away
If decency were to have a day
Then today was to be that day.

Kids met in a small group.
To take their final exam
Growth from a small group experience
Is the kind of teacher I am?

A box of donuts sat on a table.
And they were a day old
Eleven donuts sat in this box.
After a day they had grown cold

Kid one asked for a donut.
And was given permission to eat.
Another kid wanted a donut.
And a teacher took away his treat.

She yelled at him, put it back.
That does not belong to you.
I replied he was given permission.
What else is he supposed to do

Upset the kid put the donut back.
Complying with her demand
You do not have to yell at me miss.
I put it back I understand.

That is when Kid 1 broke his donut.
And gave Kid 2 the other half.
They each shared half a donut.
Decency is what I call this math.

This day the educator was wrong.
Education is special she forgot.
As a teacher we should keep in mind
There's the do's, the don'ts, and the nots.

It does not happen often.
When teachers learn from kids
Personal time vs a kid's testing time
If someone learned this day she did

Earlism (Part 3)

Technology levels the playing field. Which
side of the data base are you on?

**The problem with young coaches is that they let
emotions and egos interfere with rationality.**

Parents want to give their children the world
but should teach them how to live in it.

Can you be a librarian and not like to read?

Sometimes nothing said is more powerful than all
the words in the world. Situations will vary.

**When you are right, do not gloat. Take the small
victory. Act like you have been right before.**

Training your team to win sends a message that you are not good
enough to win. This venture is more detrimental than loosing.

**The price for excellence is demanding work. The price for
greatness is also challenging work and then do more.**

If you must brag, brag with your actions not your wallet.

When your dreams are not large enough to wake you up in the morning and drive you to do the unbelievable then your dreams are not large enough.

Forgiveness is difficult, but necessary. Not for them, but for you!

True healing begins with forgiveness authenticated by the heart.

You will watch other peers play if you cannot be coach.

The courage to stand comes from your willingness to walk!

When competing, you must do the trivial things so the grandiose things can happen.

Small thoughts will generate small efforts where versus large thoughts will yield larger efforts. Either way your efforts separate you from your peers.

If you ever have the chance to make a difference.
Make a DIFFERENCE!
The outcome is invaluable.

A humble man teaches people how to lead by the way he lives his life.

You will never appreciate your journey if someone else has to walk it for you.

Final Thoughts

Always leave things better than you found them!

Do what is right when no one else is looking!

Life is short
(Keep it simple)

Never settle on someone else's terms
if it does not benefit everyone.

Be kind! God is Watching.

Racism and protests are the foundations of the
United States of America
Embrace it, learn from it, and let's move on from it.

INDEX

A Brother Has Problems, 33
A Family Thing, 178
A Father's Love, 203
A Good Heart, 44
A Little Taste of Home, 131
A Song of Healing, 182
Acceptable, 89
Adam and Eve (The Fall of Paradise), 105
Affirmation, x
Black Forget Me-Nots, 15
Blessed Nature, 13
Candid Conversations, 162
Chapter Five:, 153
Chapter Four:, 130
Chapter One:, 1
Chapter Three:, 103
Chapter Two, 43
Chose to Learn, 118
Christian Expectation, 184
Christmas 2021, 74
Country Skies, 112
Day of Decency, 211
Deja You (RAF Alconbury), 24
Down Low, 120
E. M. Daggett Bulldogs, 58
Earlism (Part 3), 213
Easter Who, 139

Eat to Live don't Live to Eat, 135
Final Thoughts, 215
Flash and Light, 6
God Smiled, 8
Golden Bear Pride, 56
Grown Folks Stuff, 26
Handful of Man, 4
Happy Employment, 186
Hearts Do Not Lie, 38
Heaven's Lighthouse, 93
Hold On, 66
I Will Never Smile That Way Again, 133
In God's House, 156
In Memory of, 9
Infuriated as an Educator, 209
Internal Damage, 78
It Could Have Been Me, 80
Life will Happen, 149
Little Stinker, 114
Longevity's Brevity, 50
Magical Moments, 172
Mama Knew Something, 164
Moments of Discouragement, 16
My United States Air Force, 108
Names on God's List, 116
Never Wishes, 68
Non-Believers, 201

Now and Next, 60
Own Your Own Magic, 85
PREFACE, ix
Princess Sophia and Earl's Girl, 154
Quit It, 143
Remember That Story, 99
Rise and Shine, 42
Scene Standing, 40
Shoulders and Sweethearts, 70
Shrinage, 151
Silent Strength, 158
Softer Times, 87
Some People, 168
Speaking for a Friend, 174
Storybook Dreams, 207
Strength for the Strong, 205
Strong who, 97
Table of Contents, v
Talk to Me, 20
Tears of angels, 35
That Last Breath, 126
That Little Girl Christmas Spirit, 62
That Old Couch, 160
That Thing You Do, 166
That Turkey on Thanksgiving, 141
That Used to be Me, 18
The Best Sleep In The World, 48
The Black Awakening, 11
The Day You Became Who, 176
The Favor to Savor, 137
The Game of His Life, 76

The Great White Lie, 2
The Inside Man, 145
The Magic of Love, 101
The Mother of Days, 22
The Night Watcher, 14
The Other Side of Happiness, 199
The Power of Prayer, 91
The Preovulation of GOD, 188
The Privilege of Waking Up, 110
The Smell of Healing, 124
The Smell of Hickory, 128
The Time I Needed God, 180
Things I Can See, 190
Things I Know About You, 64
This Crazy Life, 147
Through The Eyes of Hate, 122
Today an Angel Went Home, 30
Today I loss a Friend, 28
Today I Saw You, 54
Touch me, Heal me, 83
Touched by Death, 52
Ultimate Loss, 197
Unknown feelings, 32
We Gone Let It Shine, 95
When a fart is a fart, 104
When Luck Has Run, 72
When We Fellowshipped, 170
Who Has You, 195
Who Knew, 193
Worth the Wisdom, 36

www.ingramcontent.com/pod-product-compliance
Lightning Source LLC
LaVergne TN
LVHW010203070526
838199LV00062B/4472